Humpback Whales

By Julie Haydon

Contents

Humpback Whales

Logbook of Jim Harris, Tour Guide

8:00 a.m.

Captain Perry of Whale Watch Adventures checked the early morning weather forecast while the crew and I completed our final checks of the tour boat. The boat was moored securely at the wharf awaiting the arrival of our first passengers for the day.

9:00 a.m.

We had 60 people including the crew on board today. As Captain Perry expertly steered the boat along the channel and out into the open sea, I took the opportunity to describe humpback whales – the magnificent creatures we were about to see.

9:30 a.m.

It wasn't long before a humpback whale was spotted. There were cries of delight from the passengers as a huge vapour cloud sprayed skywards. I explained that the whale had come to the surface to breathe out or "blow". The whale then lifted its body from the water in a gentle rolling movement.

9:35 a.m.

The passengers watched in awe as a second whale opened the two blowholes on top of its head and released another huge spray of moist breath.

9:45 a.m.

A pod of whales, including a mother with her calf, swam nearby. Captain Perry brought the boat quietly to a stop. I informed the passengers that there are rules to protect sea life. The tour boat had to stay at least 100 metres away from the whales and not block their path.

10:00 a.m.

One of the whales breached not far from us. It leapt out of the water with its belly up. As it fell backwards, the sight and sound of this huge creature hitting the water was amazing.

12:00 p.m.

On our way back to the wharf, a school of dolphins leapt and dived around the boat. Seals basking on the nearby rocks lifted their heads lazily to watch us as we passed by.

Everyone agreed it had been an excellent trip.

Gentle Giant of the Sea

Humpback whale, humpback whale,
Gentle giant of the sea,
Such mighty fins you have,
Though you're a mammal, like me.

Humpback whale, humpback whale,
Sing your changing song.
Sing a tune of beauty.
Sing on and on.

blowholes

tail

eye

body

fin

Humpback whale, humpback whale,
Of large blowholes you have two.
Come up to the surface
To breathe air is what you do.

Humpback whale, humpback whale,
Sing your changing song.
Lie still in the water.
Sing on and on.

Humpback whale, humpback whale,
Small fish and krill are your prey.
Gulp big mouthfuls of food,
While the water drains away.

Humpback whale, humpback whale,
Sing your changing song
Of moans and groans and cries.
Sing on and on.

Humpback whale, humpback whale,
You're found in every ocean.
Polar seas in summer.
Winter sets you in motion.

Humpback whale, humpback whale,
Sing your changing song,
As you swim all alone,
Sing on and on.

Humpback whale, humpback whale,
Swim to warmer seas to breed.
Birth your giant calf there,
And make milk so it can feed.

Humpback whale, humpback whale,
Sing your changing song.
Why is it that you sing?
Sing on and on.

Humpback whale, humpback whale,
High out of the sea you leap.
Face your belly skywards,
Fall back to the ocean deep.

Humpback whale, humpback whale,
Sing your changing song.
If it makes you happy,
Sing on and on.